Cruising at Sixty to Seventy

Cruising at Sixty to Seventy

poems and essay

Jim Tilley

RED HEN PRESS | *Pasadena, CA*

Cruising at Sixty to Seventy: Poems and Essay

Book design and layout by Jaimie Evans

ISBN 978-1-59709-536-5 (tradepaper)

ISBN 978-1-59709-264-7 (clothbound)

Library of Congress Cataloging-in-Publication Data

Tilley, Jim.

[Works. Selections]

Cruising at sixty to seventy : poems and essay / Jim Tilley.—First Edition.

pages cm

I. Title.

PS3620.I515C78 2014

811'.6—dc23

2013033338

The National Endowment for the Arts, the Los Angeles County Arts Commission, the Los Angeles Department of Cultural Affairs, the Dwight Stuart Youth Fund, the Pasadena Arts & Cultural Commission and the City of Pasadena Cultural Affairs Division and Sony Pictures Entertainment partially support Red Hen Press.

First Edition

Published by Red Hen Press

www.redhen.org

Acknowledgments

Grateful acknowledgment is made to the following journals in which certain poems in this book first appeared, sometimes under different titles and/or in previous versions.

Alaska Quarterly Review: "Billy and Stephen and Me"; *Atlanta Review*: "Learning to Write"; *BigCityLit.com*: "Aftermath," "Cruising at Sixty to Seventy"; *Cimarron Review*: "Your Reality After All"; *Comstock Review*: "Man in Day-Glo Yellow"; *Hawai'i Pacific Review*: "New Road"; *Hotel Amerika*: "Anniversary," "Order in the Universe," "Winter Jacket"; *Hurricane Review*: "Biorhythms"; *Lascaux Review*: "At Least One Point"; *New Orleans Review*: "Ceci n'est pas une armoire," "Problem #193," "Two of Them"; *Oberon Poetry*: "Yesterday's Questions"; *Poet Lore*: "Particle and Wave"; *Poetry East*: "Figure Skating," "The Log"; *River Styx*: "Ode to a Martini," "Ode to Leaves"; *Southwest Review*: "The Drought"; *Tar River Poetry*: "Croccantini Crackers," "Morning Calculus," "Timothy"; *The Tower Review*: "At Sewanee," "Earthworm," "New Balance," "Quantum Computing"; and *Virginia Quarterly Review*: "Remembrance Day, 11/11/11."

"Learning to Write" won an International Publication Award from *Atlanta Review*.

"At Least One Point" was nominated for the *Best of the Net 2012* anthology.

"Hello, Old Man" will appear in a forthcoming edition of *Poetry: An Introduction* (Bedford/St. Martin's), edited by Michael Meyer.

Twenty-eight poems in this collection, all under different titles and some in previous versions, constituted a manuscript, "Cruising at Sixty to Seventy: Hamish's Diary Poems," which was a finalist for *Tupelo Press*'s 2012 Snowbound Chapbook Award.

"The Elegant Solution" was published by *Ploughshares* both in e-book form as No. 7 in their Solo Series and in print form as part of an anthology of short stories and essays.

I want to thank my poet colleagues Will Wells, Charles Coté, and James Scruton for their critiques of the essay and several of the poems in this collection, and my wife and agent, Deborah Schneider, who is a tireless reader and reviewer of all my work and a source of constant encouragement.

for my wife, Deborah C. Schneider

Contents

I. Poems—Dear Wife

Winter Jacket 17
Morning Calculus 18
Biorhythms 20
New Balance 22
Ceci n'est pas une armoire 23
Two of Them 24
Particle and Wave 26
Croccantini Crackers 27
Learning to Write 28
Problem #193 29
Quantum Computing 30
Aftermath 32
Timothy 33
Anniversary 34

II. Poems—Dear Self

Trading Up 39
Artifact 40
Order in the Universe 42
Of Democritus and Heraclitus 44
Another Man's Towel 46
Hello, Old Man 48
Winding Down 49
Remembrance Day, 11/11/11 50
At Least One Point 52
Walking by Numbers 54

New Road 57
Cruising at Sixty to Seventy 58
At Sewanee 60
The Log 61

III. Poems—Dear Friends

The Farmer's Daffodils 65
Man in Day-Glo Yellow 66
Billy and Stephen and Me 68
Ode to Leaves 69
Your Reality After All 70
Delayed 72
Tadpole 73
The Swan Song of Mr. Bullfrog 74
Drought 76
Earthworm 78
Yesterday's Questions 79
Passion Lies Down 80
Ode to a Martini 82
Figure Skating 83

IV. Essay

The Elegant Solution 87

One starts to get young at the age of sixty, and then it is too late.

—Pablo Picasso

Cruising at Sixty to Seventy

I. Poems—Dear Wife

Winter Jacket

Divorced for two years, he's been dating a new woman for one. Last night over the dinner she made, he told her about his walk that morning on which he'd found a child's winter jacket hanging on a fencepost and hadn't been able to figure out how it got there. She imagined a boy riding alone in the back seat of a car, who felt hot, took off his jacket, then heaved it out the window and giggled, not realizing what he'd thrown away. Someone like you out for a walk picked it up from the edge of the road and fastened it to the post. Simple, she said. Not really, he said. Cars have child-locked windows, and even if the parents forgot, they would have caught their son in the act and stopped the car. Unless they were arguing again—it leaves its marks, doesn't it? she said. Don't want that, he said. Sometime when you find yourself traveling the same road, she said, you might see a person holding out your lost jacket as you're about to pass by. Like this, she said.

Morning Calculus

Since you claim it was given by your son
to you, not me, my goal before I die
is to have you understand all the formulas
inscribed on that cup you place
your hands around every morning

to raise to your nostrils to breathe
the day-awakening scent of fresh-ground
French roast—the lives of skyscrapers
and suspension bridges erected on that calculus,
telecommunication satellites slung into

orbits defined by those equations, a system
of spherical coordinates to help us
navigate our non-Cartesian, non-orthogonal,
non-x-y-z world. Well, maybe not
the transformation of a multi-dimensional

integral under a change of variables,
its Jacobian not a determinant of anything
that ever was or will be between us.
For now, it will suffice for me to have you
note that $x^2 + y^2 = z^2$ is not only

the right-angled creation of an ancient
Pythagorean mind, but also the surfaces
of mirror-image cones somewhat wider
than the ones your father used to buy
for each of you as you ambled the lakefront

fifty years ago, vanilla ice cream dripping
down the sticky fingers of the hand
now gripping the mug covered with
markings you may never understand, a hand
no equation could ever describe.

Biorhythms

before a line by Archibald MacLeish

Early on, he favored essay questions,
but they quickly evolved into short answers,
then multiple choice. After years,
he's learned the key to success
throughout the daily daylong test.

In the morning, he reads the sports section,
waits thirty minutes before speaking
to allow the coffee to fully stir
her dormant alpha waves,
then always asks how her first answer
differs from her second.

Around noon, he senses when she settles
into her usual pattern of
A. Gut instinct
B. Detailed analysis
C. Doubt and re-examination
and catches himself changing his guesses.

By late afternoon, he sees her eyes
scanning for traces of his lingering indecision,
those incomplete erasures
that hang in the air and betray him.
He seeks safe harbor in *D. All of the above,*
compliments her on presenting
an attractive array of options.

As evening wears on,
he discovers that *E. None of the above*
is actually optimal. It's clear he's absorbed
nothing. Nothing. Nothing at all.

New Balance

God was wearing his New Balance 991s
when he stepped out of the house to run with his wife
and pulled up short on the driveway
where a mouse was twitching on its side
as if to scratch an unrelenting itch.
"Oh God!" she said, "It's the chemical I sprayed
between the cobblestones. Please put it out of its misery."
And God, tired of glyphosate in the world
and discrimination against weeds
because he'd made them, too, wanted to
be cross with her. What's done is done, she'd say,
though he could still change many things.
Knowing he could not heal the mouse,
he placed the shadow of his right shoe over the creature
and stepped down hard. Better than
the old days when he'd been an angrier god
driven by moods. He remembers the nightmares
in the time before he set up rules, and how
the migraines disappeared when he no longer had to
judge everything himself. Things are easier now—
now that he's used to doing as he's told.

Ceci n'est pas une armoire

She had sketched a bowler hat in black—
the same as on those men raining
out of the sky—in the upper left-hand corner
of her full-page drawing. Beneath it
a pipe that wasn't a pipe. She even forged
his signature in the lower right-hand corner
in case I'd forgotten where the iconic
images came from. She wrote in French
she knew I'd understand. Placed it on my
favorite chair—antique sitting piece on casters
by the window in the corner of our bedroom,
re-upholstered hunt green with a host
of birds, rabbits, dogs and leaping deer—
a spot I seldom sit but often put the clothes
I shed during the day and just before bed,
sometimes folding and stacking them
in a neat pile, also the fresh clothes
I lay out to wear the next morning
whenever I know I'll be leaving in the dark
while she's asleep. The armchair
in her sketch is orange, the only colored
marker she had handy I suppose, her favorite
red gone missing or spent. Her this-is-not-
a-closet chair placed on the chair that is indeed
a chair, but also a symbol of what's
the same between us in this marriage—
good humor, French, a love of art—
and what's different, the perception of when
something has found its proper place.

Two of Them

Two of them on a bare branch
chattering at each other again—
sometimes in turn, sometimes both at once
one over the other as if talking
to an unseen, higher bird,
arbiter for opposing points of view.

Perhaps they're both exclaiming,
in their own not always
compatible ways, how fine
the morning is shaping up, not a cloud,
the sun only now making an appearance
over the far hills, light spreading
inward through the valley.

Have they mastered the art
of completing each other's thoughts?
Is that a flush of irritation
in the one interrupted,
who had hoped, for once,
to complete her own—

the one who had wanted to agree
that today's daybreak is magnificent
though not like yesterday's,
which could have been a painting
by a famous artist at the turn of the century
when it seemed there were fewer birds

in the world, fewer fiefdoms,
fewer nests cluttering the treetops,
the air itself less frenetic,
when birds not only sang but heard,
when mates found it easier
to share the same space for life?

Particle and Wave

particles have no meaning as isolated entities,
but can only be understood as interconnections . . .
—Erwin Schrödinger

You and I were doing what we do best—
throwing stones—
this time from the side
of a country bridge into the reservoir,
each arcing under the forces
of physics until impact, the consequence
spreading in ripples, the stone
become invisible in the bottom muck,
its presence propagating
across the surface,
as our presence does
to the fabric of something less grand
than space-time. Then yours and mine
cast together, landing in different spots,
their wavelets colliding,
passing through each other,
cohering in some places, canceling in others,
the pattern richer for the two
than one . . .   then in our excitement,
each of us tossing a handful at once,
the pattern becoming richer still,
not still at all, moving out into the world—
children, siblings, parents, friends,
adding up to something grand.

Croccantini Crackers

Not so much yesterday's phone call, but the forecasted
arrival of Hurricane Earl changed the plans—
our fisherman friend decided to haul his boat onto land,

take his chances with toppling trees. So now instead
of picnicking on Monomoy, our annual retreat, we're
lunching by his salt-water pool. But there's still

the chilled wine and this year's hit—scallop pâté
smeared on bite-size pieces we break off in random shapes
from sheets of Croccantini crackers. My wife says

hers looks like Virginia, mine like Iowa. Sometimes
we happen to make a long, thin Tennessee, but never
a Texas. Never an Illinois—that would remind us

of the sister just diagnosed with Stage IV lesions
in the brain and lung. We changed but didn't cancel plans.
Too early for that. Next year perhaps. Today,

no matter the state of things, a menu of ease,
new boundaries, but no battles. Crackers, pâté. Calm
before the storm more than the eye of the hurricane,

a remission we will pray for. Now—right now—
a moment when taste is allowed to trump almost anything;
tomorrow, the work of clearing away what we can.

Learning to Write

—for DonnaLee

Her left hand grasps the fat, soft-leaded pencil,
makes broad strokes between the wide-ruled lines
that tops and bottoms of characters must barely
touch, those smooth cursive loops, curls,
arcs and straight parts, double-size for capitals,
letter by letter through the alphabet.

A lifetime of experience tells her she has choices—
the modern-style, lower-case "r" she learned
in grade school or the old-fashioned one with cusps
at the peaks of its ascending and descending edges,
the kind to which she switched in high school
after reading her sister's letters from college.
The letter "p" she used to leave open the way
the Sisters taught her, but now feels a need to close,
always retracing her path before moving on.

She's slow and awkward and her script isn't
beautiful yet, not like the copperplate gothic
before her right-hand tremors,
before her husband had to shave her head
after radiation took away her shoulder-length red hair.
Now she can see the smooth curves of her ears
holding the diamond studs he gave her last birthday.
Now her thank-you notes have a different slant.

Problem #193

It was Banach's wife who gave them the journal
they called *The Scottish Book* so they wouldn't
keep losing the solutions they wrote on the marble
tabletops in the Scottish Café, those famous

mathematicians in Lvov who kept a log
of the solvable and unsolvable, as you do now
in your journal with the marble pattern on its cover.
I've been thinking about Problem #193,

Banach's puzzle involving a mathematician
who carries two boxes of matches,
one in his left pocket and one in his right,
each with M matches at the start. To light his pipe,

he chooses a box at random, removes a match
and strikes it. Does this every time until he finds
one of the boxes is empty. But how would he know?
When he reaches for another match and finds

the box bare? I've been thinking this could be us.
Not the times we're lying in bed bantering,
when you keep talking into the silence until you
realize my last match has already been spent

and you still have N things to tell me. It's after
another fight has burned down almost to silence,
when you wonder aloud whether we began
with equal amounts each. Whether anything's left.

Quantum Computing

Have you read the *New Yorker* article?

It told me nothing I don't know.

Do you know what you don't understand?

It's not as if you do or you don't.

So what's the problem?

I think I understand you and know I don't.

You don't even understand yourself.

I know you live in too many worlds.

And you're forever trying to find your own.

Aren't I always tangled up in you?

Only when we're together.

The article says even when we're apart.

It's harder when we're together.

Do we have to talk in qubits like this?

That's how it says to solve our problems.

You mean we're stuck in this state—

—of being both turned on and off? . . . Yes.

Are you sure that's necessary?

Not for me—I only ever have one problem.

You might still need qubits for that.

Aftermath

Why this particular Cleveland pear? What takes
a cherry instead of a plum? Oversized wet flakes

thick in the air, that but for a few degrees would be rain,
settle on still-green leaves, accumulate, strain

branches and trunks. And like people, some break.
In rising wind, a night of cracking. We lie awake.

At dawn, we find splintered limbs littering the lawn,
whole maples down, beeches with their centers gone.

The melt begins, too late. Will birches continue to weep
or lift themselves? Should we cut down or keep

the English oak? Its tendril branches, now unfurled,
no longer hug the trunk; raised arms that swirled

like a figure skater's locked in a spin
hang limp. It may take years for them to fill back in.

Everywhere uprooted shrubs. What to do with a yard
that a Nor'easter has disfigured into a ward

of fresh amputees? Move the debris out of sight
into the woods? It wouldn't make things right,

but we could leave the rest till spring, give the broken
a certain grace. Let this grief remain unspoken.

Timothy

What is hay made from? you ask. I want to say
          we should forget talk,

make it back home before the darkening gray
          turns to rain, but you are serious. You pick a stalk.

How about this? you ask. It isn't the type
          of wild grass I knew when I was young,

brushing through fields of it, tall and dense, almost ripe
          by the end of June. The kind the tongue

finds sweet, whose head looks like a miniature cattail.
          I'd hold one, pinching it near the tip

between thumb and forefinger, and, almost without fail,
          using those digits of the other hand, strip

the seeds in one smooth stroke. And now,
          fifty years later, farther along the road, a scant row

bends in the wind. We each take one. This is how
          it's done, I say, though I suspect you already know.

Anniversary

From the solace of a hot shower beating
on my shoulders and back, through
the misted glass doors out into
the bathroom and beyond
its wall of windows, I discern bands of clouds
peeling from the horizon
heading this way, making alternating strips
of light and shadow that sweep across
the layers of wooded hills
barren of leaves . . .   beyond all that
the interior

                    monologue I can't wash away,
the words you gave voice to this morning
about the bands of light and shadow
that constantly sweep across my mind,
always more shadow than light,
the good I do not good enough
to do me enough good, but this time I gave you
time to deliver your monologue
about the help I need to give myself
that would bring the greatest gift
I could give to you.

                                        Then you left,
and after sitting in the hunt chair
by the window of our bedroom a while,
I left, too,

to take this shower and watch
layer upon layer of shadow
make their uninvited way into the room
and come to me. With my fingers splayed,
I wiped away the mist so I could
see more clearly, feel the waves pass through,
not knowing what else to do.
Everything misted up again, and you—

you passed by the doorway, I thought,
or your shadow did.

II. Poems—Dear Self

Trading Up

He tells himself it was time to pull the plug though she'd been with him every day for years, gone everywhere he asked, given him stories, left countless letters and notes, messages, sometimes even those he had to hear. She'd made him reply when it was important, kept him up to date on happenings in his world and beyond, watched over his failing portfolio, even helped him find where he was or wanted to go. She could do things he didn't even know. She brought color and flash into his life. But he wore her down, and, try as she might, she couldn't seem to sustain her energy long enough to satisfy him. So now he's let her go, found someone new, "an uptick," he says, someone who can talk to him, asks what he wants, senses his desires, but always checks first before doing something he might not approve. He knows she'll save him from trying to do everything himself. And though there are certain things she'll never be able to accomplish, no matter how much he pleads or cajoles, she improves his life and he knows he'll keep her—at least for a while, until she, too, wears out or someone better comes along.

Artifact

Sent away because his wife said he should
find someone who didn't mind being owned,
he is here alone, on a terrace

waiting for the sky to brighten over the town of Cortona
veiled in haze from brush fires
in the olive groves, thinking about

his visit yesterday to the ruins of the Roman
amphitheater in Arezzo, where he spent
an hour at the museum looking at Etruscan

artifacts that made him feel old.
On the way out, he paused to examine an exhibit
of photographs, everything for sale,

including a picture of a young woman
sitting on the floor beneath a window, knees
drawn nearly to her chest, legs

tantalizingly apart, pulling his eyes to the spot
where she holds a large fragment of a mirror
reflecting an image of herself from another

mirror, an endless chain of what he imagined
lay behind his malaise. Then he noticed her face,
head turned slightly, eyes closed.

He imagined those eyes gazing into his,
inviting him into the frame. So he brought her here,
to the villas at Il Falconiere,

where she lies upstairs, still sleeping, he supposes,
like his wife, while he sits alone
in a haze, waiting for the sky to brighten.

Order in the Universe

Another of those big questions, existential matter,
    order in the universe, my own
more than the imponderable
    theory of everything, the selfish me
for once worrying about my spouse
    and children, imbalance in their worlds

creating disequilibrium in mine; I search for
    signs everywhere, markers I've established,
components of an index of my well-being.
    We all do, don't we?
Must disorder in someone else's universe
    mean disarray in yours? It may be of no

consequence to you how the universe came to be
    or whether we inhabit one of many,
whether the finest of strings hold us together
    as a universe if not a race,
play the music of our spheres, but it is to me.
    Unable to decipher the dark

energy pulling us apart, I find myself
    pulled back into the solipsistic world of me,
the failures of others becoming my own,
    even my favorite team's loss
in the finals of the league championship
    an omen of something sinister, my stock

portfolio unable to recover its losses by next week
        or next year. Instead, I know it will
continue its fall, but not far enough to hit
        my buy-limit order, GTC, the kind of order
I'd order for my universe, if only I could.
        Good-Till-Cancelled. Solely by me.

Of Democritus and Heraclitus

A gift, this Teeter Hang-Ups
Body Inverter, Model EP-950, easy to assemble
once the required parts have been organized,
spread out on the floor, each ready to find
its rightful spot. Usually it's the discovery
that a piece is missing that grinds everything

to a halt, not the presence of damn double-
threaded bolts like these GL-9523s, their proper
insertion into the A-frame's arms not possible
to ascertain from the diagram's dotted lines.
Easier to follow was Essay #50, which I read
while lying on my stomach, until my back

began to throb. Democritus appeared
a few pages in, perched high on a boulder,
offering advice, but laughing in anticipation
of my attempt at betterment, Heraclitus
a few pages farther on, leaning against a tree,
doing one better—weeping at the futility,

even before learning what I would be up against—
and near the end, Montaigne himself,
evidently inclined toward Democritus, agreeing
that it's an animal's lack of imagination
that keeps it happy, thinking of bats I suppose,
they, too, hanging upside down when their wings

become too heavy to bear. Then their backs
stop aching. That's why this is a gift,
or will be soon. But Democritus is wrong—
bats are happy only because they arrive with
the required apparatus intact, no need to follow
directions, no need to read between the lines.

Another Man's Towel

M'aidez. M'aidez. M'aidez.
Three times the cock crows
to signify the standard protocol,
Frenchman sinking on a May day
in the middle of Manhattan.

Wrapped in a towel, I sit on a barstool
with the Sunday newspaper
to keep me warm,
eating a bowl of cornflakes
sprinkled with blackberries, savoring

the early report of the man
I allow myself to become, naked
in front of the hotel chambermaid,
thinking of groping her
and a deeper pleasure,

something beyond the juice
of succulent blackberries
out here under the gazebo,
a man on the edge
after a hot shower, drying off,

taking a last look at the city,
open suitcase at his feet as he contemplates
his flight, imagines a more
flattering portrait,
head tilted to a different angle,

nose casting a lesser shadow,
hair streaked silver instead of gray,
a man interrupted from his reverie,
dropping the towel,
chasing, tackling, pressing

his knees against thighs, pinning
wrists to the coldness of the floor.
The art of the hunt, everything
brushed over in broad, sweeping strokes,
swaths fresh and thick, black . . .

and there they are, outside the frame
watching the past fast-forward,
managing director/presidential hopeful
who chose a life under the lights,
and his chambermaid who maybe did not.

Hello, Old Man

"Hello, old man," a voice called out as I
passed by the Kenter Canyon Charter School.
I paused and chuckled. "Hello back," I said
to the girl on the playground swing, knowing
it might be fifty years before she'd understand.
Unrestrained in expressing what they see,
the young are often right. She'd seen white hair.
But for me that day striding up the canyon's
steep hill, four miles into my morning walk,
old age was only a state of mind—
or almost so. Right before the school,
I'd detoured onto a quiet side street
and climbed among some bushes, having spent
the last mile looking for a place to pee.

Winding Down

A book or magazine tented on his chest, he snoozes
on the recliner on-and-off until mid-morning unless
it's one of those days he leaves at nine, drives himself
to the Senior Center for the tai chi class he used to teach,
yet always home for the lunch she makes for them,
always served on a white plate—Coleslaw, chick peas,
cottage cheese, chunks of tuna, cut-up bits of tomato,
bowl of split pea or lentil or carrot or broccoli soup—
then a longer nap while she works on her crosswords
and number puzzles, reads the latest romance novel
or drives off to line dance class where she now shares
the teaching with someone younger with less arthritis,
back in time for their soap opera, after which dinner,
one of several she no longer makes from scratch,
something frozen, thawed and baked, with the meal's
allotment of pills for each, glass of cheap Pinot for him,
tap water for her to wash them down, both sitting
in front of the TV watching the national and local news,
him dozing again while she scrubs the day's dishes
before they listen to a CD of their favorite music,
skip through songs they don't like, retire for the night
to regenerate the routine that begins with the same
breakfast, him recording his weight, her collecting
the newspapers and later the mail, until time runs out
at this modest house at river's edge with its dandelion-
free yard and water always lapping against the rocks.

Remembrance Day, 11/11/11

Uniform and medals in place, he began to recite:
        We few, we happy few, we band of brothers . . .
I let him continue, word for word to the end,
        pausing only for proper punctuation.
Perfect, just as in his prep school days. Blue ribbon.
        Forest of Compiègne, I said. Not Agincourt.
We are the Dead. Short days ago
        We lived, felt dawn, saw sunset glow . . .
He proceeded through the rest of Flanders Fields alone.
        I asked, Can the dead be happy?,

knowing, as I always do, what he'll say:
        Not unless they see sunrise and sunset.
At eleven, the sun was almost as high as it would get.
        They remembered my father
at the chapel, asked how he was doing.
        And as he had the year before, he told them
about his days in flight training, the time
        he flew over his prep school's football field,
almost touching down, almost not making it
        back up, goalposts nearly nicking a wing.

Back then, Henry V was firmly in his place,
        Lieutenant Colonel McCrae too,
but not me, not even an inkling though he knew
        his bride-to-be. Hey, Dad, do you remember
meeting Mum? I asked, and he joked:
        When they heard I'd been given a commission,
they surrendered. So did she, I thought.
        When we came out after the service, we saw

that clouds had gathered on the day,
the sun strafing them in a few spots.

Over a spot of lunch, we talked about what he could
remember, pockets of recollection
in odd places and times, his unusual condition unkindly
rendering some of the unforgettable lost
while leaving much of the forgettable found.
He recalled the birthday gift for his brother
who guessed what it was after he'd asked and was told
only that it looked like a hammer.
I asked if he recalled hiking with me, navigations
by means of compass and map to find

unnamed mountain ponds he could call his own.
He still did. And also the time he and his brother
set a field of brush ablaze with their father's
magnifying glass. But not the birth of his son
on the coldest day on record or the party at which
he met my mother who'd come with
another man. After an early tea, we drove to the lake
and watched the sky's coals burn down.
He began to recite *Henry V* again.
It was Saint Crispin's Day. He was king.

At Least One Point

My father always wanted to own an island,
but settled for unnamed ponds
to which he could affix his name for all time.
Armed with compass and large-scale map,
we'd set out in search of those tiny
spots of blue, trying to reach them
before the sun set early in the mountains.
We'd stand at the edge of his discoveries,
linger until there was barely time
to make it back before dark. Hurrying along,
we scrambled through brambles,
slipped on mossy rocks in brooks
as night squeezed out the forest's last light.

One afternoon, frustrated as we kept failing
to find the dot of water the map claimed
was there, losing the battle against
the topography of the place, he thought I might
prefer the challenge of topology instead,
and said, "There is a mountain trail.
You leave the base at eight in the morning
and reach the peak at eight at night,
start back down at eight the next morning,
return to the base at eight that night.
Prove that there is at least one point in time
when you're at the same point on the trail
each day, whether you stop at a stream to drink,
pause to pick newly ripened raspberries,
lie down to contemplate clouds, or not."

My father never settled for clumsy solutions,
some leap of insight always required,
a transformation to an equivalent problem
easy to solve. I couldn't have said,
"Two continuous graphs in the x-y plane,
one for the way up, one for the way down,
must intersect at at least one point."
No—it had to be two people on the same day,
one heading up, the other coming down,
destined to cross paths along the way.

Now that my father is old, I offer
the elegant solution as father and son
meeting somewhere along their journeys—
like my son's ascent and my decline
twenty years hence, he looking up at me
standing at the precipice of dementia
looking down, as I stand now looking up.

Walking by Numbers

At first glance, there's nothing special
about the number 11461,
address of The Luxe on Sunset Boulevard,
except a prime location to start
a walk westward through Brentwood,

past the public school hiding behind tall hedges,
past the white-stucco, clay-tile roof,
two-story Archer School for Girls
with its wall of bougainvillea,
far enough to determine that 11461 isn't prime,

but the product of 53 and 157, each a prime.
For no reason other than the elegance
in arithmetic progressions, the number 12345
becomes the target destination,
arriving too soon, nice enough house in a row

of nice enough houses with so-so lawns,
nothing spectacularly prime along this stretch.
An embankment makes the no-sidewalk
north side at Cliffwood too dangerous to walk,
too dangerous for Julia, whose memorial

bench, painted purple with flowers,
warns passersby to slow down, reminds them
that their days, too, are finite and numbered.
The scene changes as the boulevard loops
around sports fields at the Revere Middle School,

its lot filled with Los Angeles Unified
School District buses, students milling in groups
before the opening bell, active games
under eleven of the twelve hoops,
a thin black boy chatting up a buxom white girl

through a chain-link fence while friends
harangue him to start the game or hand over
the ball. The school's drab exterior
is marked with an arrow indicating "X building"
to the left. Across the high-walled spillway

with its trickle of runoff, a cluster of kids—
Latino, Asian, Black and White—
who likely don't care what X stands for,
not seeing the point to mathematics
other than the dollars and cents needed to bridge

today to tomorrow. Past the school and row
of jacarandas dropping their blue corollas
are Monaco and Capri, entrance to the Riviera
Country Club, opposite where 13579
should be but isn't. On the way back,

it will take a while to figure out
that the missing address is also a product
of two primes. Time enough to strip
a fistful of powdery Eucalyptus leaves,
no thought of counting them

because the exact number will not matter,
not a sign of any imbalance in the world if odd,
nor indication that what's beautiful
and what's not are inseparable
parts of a whole if prime. They have

a pleasing scent, one to pervade a room
where there will be nothing to do but ponder
why St. Martin of Tours Catholic Church
with its parochial school and silo bell tower
has no boundary hedge or fence,

while right across the street, University Synagogue
is protected by cinderblock and steelbar walls,
Maximum Security System signs
planted in the garden to keep people out
and providing the number to call if they don't.

New Road

They're busy out on the road, this parade of heavy
equipment. For a week I've watched these guys
while I wait for my son to return from overseas—
a month without news. Every day at 5:30 am,

I've listened to the mammoth grader squeal along
the stripped-down road shearing off stones. Today,
a man leans from a slowly moving truck placing pylons.
Others stand around with coffee and rolls. I ask about

those stakes at regular intervals with Styrofoam plates
stapled to them, signs marked by hand +4, +2, 0, -2, . . .
It's how the road is banked at bends, the foreman says.
They're constantly making adjustments by degrees.

That's what I do, now that my son has graduated
and is looking for work. All preparations finished,
a long narrow truck drops its tarry mix into a machine
that inches along, laying down a one-lane section

of new road, careful to stay aligned with the orange
shoulder markings, steamrollers queued up behind it,
ready to render everything firm and flat, mile after mile.
Not too hard when you already know where it goes.

Cruising at Sixty to Seventy

Not that it's a herd thundering
toward the unseen edge of a precipice—
there are consequences
to plunging over a cliff with hundreds

landing on top of you after your body thuds—
but that's what I'm thinking
as I watch cars on the other side of the Interstate
cruising at sixty to seventy, nobody

realizing that right around the bend
the traffic has come to a dead stop for miles.
They're surfing radio stations, looking for
music they love or news they can tolerate,

or on the phone arguing with their bosses,
engaged in something they're accustomed to.
They likely wouldn't want to be warned,
nothing to do about missed appointments,

few once-in-a-lifetime opportunities
slipping away. Just turned sixty, on my way
to seventy, cruising without a thought
about what lies ahead, I wouldn't want

to be informed either. I haven't yet spent hours
moving nowhere today—I have all the time
I need to get where I'm going, and I'm listening
to a book on CD, *Remarkable Creatures,*

learning about an ichthyosaurus
being chiseled out of a limestone cliff,
imagining myself uncovered, discovered
after millions of years, bones turned to stone.

At Sewanee

At first it might seem that he's skirting
the issue by taking the Perimeter Trail,
even with rocks and fallen trees to cross,
rattlers to be wary of during their
molting season—they, too, dealing with
the new and bigger thing of themselves.
Yet, as he sits on a flat-topped boulder,
feet dangling over the edge, say the bluff
at Piney Point or Dotson or Elliott's,
as he watches the sun slowly pour itself
down distant mountains, the fog burn off
the plains below, he sees that it's clearer
than he thought it was, this thing that brought
him here, this thing he's trying to figure out.

The Log

Nothing to do but slump against the log, let his heart slow, try to talk himself down, make it back. He'd had to straddle it, let his front leg dangle, pull his back leg over. As he jumped to the ground, he wasn't aware of anything but a stab in his calf. A rattlesnake slithered off. He sat, oddly calm, his mind molting as the sun began to poke through the sassafras and dapple the forest floor, cicadas winding themselves up in the morning heat, the growing concert making it harder to concentrate. Live in the moment, his wife had said, and in a way this was a good moment, everything around him at peace, even the snake. But he had to write it all down while he still had some mind to. He removed a crumpled sheet of paper from his left pocket, rummaged around his right and found he'd forgotten a pen.

III. Poems—Dear Friends

The Farmer's Daffodils

Winter's claws are still digging deep into spring's flesh, but don't tell the eager farmer setting out to plow his frozen fields. Don't tell the daffodils blooming outside his stone wall. Tell the woman without a coat who parked her cruiser in the middle of the road, engine running, door ajar. Stop to ask why she knelt and cut off a bunch. Ask why she's stealing the beauty of the place, and tell her that farther down the road, someone dumped an armchair, a surplus roll of wall-to-wall carpet, and a mattress onto the hill's bed of leaves. Make sure to tell her she should leave on a note of grace, scribble a note saying she picked a mix of yellow and white, which her mother likes so much. Don't—not even for a moment—consider asking if she might be the farmer's wife.

Man in Day-Glo Yellow

He'd be a crossing guard
if there were anywhere to cross to,
old man in a reflective vest and standard issue
policeman's hat and light blue shirt

with the flag stitched onto its right sleeve.
He's there in the morning with his
hand-held stop sign to freeze the bustle
when school opens, and in the afternoon

when it lets out. You get the sense
he's an old poet, a certain rhythm
to his motions with the sign
and elegance in his back-and-forth amble

between the corner and the middle of the street.
But mostly it's the furrowed face
and gray ponytail cinched with a band—
you can see him reading to a group

of parents and students, teachers and bus drivers.
Imagine the stories, his thoughts
after a day's work as he walks back
to the apartment complex on the other side

of the tracks. He's the kind you think
it would be interesting to meet and talk to,
but you've never seen anyone do that,
pressed as everyone is to get past each other

when made to come to a full stop and wait,
grumbling under the breath about being
held back like school children, having forgotten
how to suffer the world with grace.

Billy and Stephen and Me

—for Billy Collins and Stephen Dunn

Billy would tell you about the little flame
at the end of his pen while he rocks in the hammock
listening to wild turkeys rustle last autumn's leaves
as they run toward and away from the stream.

Stephen would tell you he's like the turkeys,
unsure whether he's coming or going,
how that confusion has a certain beauty
which can't be uprooted once it takes hold, and I—

I'm the one in the hammock, reading both
on this first warm day of spring, coming from one
to the other, going back, pausing every few pages
to let the words plant themselves,

and thinking how hard it was last fall
to drill holes in each urn's composite base
so this year's flowers wouldn't drown—
likely red, white, and pink impatiens again,

because habits don't break easily
and those flowers crave shade. Billy would say
there's too much shade in the world,
Stephen that we cast too much on ourselves.

Ode to Leaves

Sidewalk strewn after wind and rain,
its cement stenciled with leaves,
stains that will last beyond the next
storm and the next, color-bearing juices
leaching out, last hurrahs as the leaves
exit the world under footsteps and sun
into skeletons of veins that crumble
to dust, a little mulch for next year's

leaves that will look exactly the same—
ovate, cordate, pinnate, spear-shaped,
sword-shaped, rhomboid, lobed—
no generation leaving anything behind,
nothing learned, nothing written down
but buds for next year's crop
to pilfer the sun, do the hard work
of adding pith to core inside the cork.

Their world is pure—never a runoff
for high office, top leaf in town,
no special deals for oak or maple,
nothing under the table, no hanky-panky
in the canopy, just birch to birch,
ash to ash. Simple: leaves like clouds
hanging around, giving shade, sometimes
billowing out, sometimes raining down.

Your Reality After All

Mindful that a mindless exercise can be therapeutic,
let's try replacing the triangle that's on your mind
with matchsticks—matchsticks to make triangles,
not to stay warm, not like the poor little Match Girl
huddling against a wall, who sees a shooting star
and wants to follow her grandmother's soul, striking

match after match to keep the vision burning,
not matchsticks to light a fire under cauldrons of soup
for the homeless on a snow-laden night, not even matchsticks
to ignite a broomstick's straw kindling, its witch tied
to a stake, because there's too much at stake when three
make a triangle—your wife and an erstwhile friend,

and you, at the vertices of something new. Burn those two
and start again. Take it down to one, but not like
the Match Girl trying to stay alive. Strike it against
the walls of Marabar's Caves and bring the struck one close
to his reflection. Perhaps your friend, if you haven't
burned him yet, will learn something about two

becoming one, or perhaps you will. Not matchsticks
to kindle the fire in your heart or the one in Plato's Cave
projecting shadows across the wall, someone else's
reality, not yours. Until you solve it, my friend,
your reality is the distraction of the puzzle here posed:
use six matchsticks to make exactly four equal equilateral

triangles. As if one weren't enough, you say, as if
you're some old Greek geometer pushing those sticks
around a tabletop in search of new directions,
only able to make two triangles with one stick unused,
or, using all, one atop another upside down—easy there—
to form a hexagram, shooting star, yellow hex

upon those winter coats, ashes to ashes, dust to dust.
History never lies, though some refuse to believe.
No, not those. Think not of yourself, but King Khufu,
no ashes, whole body wrapped, interred at Giza in his Great
Pyramid. And here you are interred in a triangle. But
how much easier to rebuild a marriage than build

a pyramid, to build a pyramid from matchsticks than
limestone blocks, merely four for the base, four for the sides,
admittedly eight not six. By now you must be thinking
3-D, and it won't be long before your neurons ignite
an Archimedean moment and you shout out. And that
would be that, wouldn't it? But what will you

shout? Surely not "Eureka!" or "Tetrahedron!"
There's no blinding insight for your problem, my friend,
the one struck in your head, the triangle that burst into flame
one night that you can't put out, the one with two
in the cave becoming one that casts too many shadows
against your walls—of late, your reality after all.

Delayed

They say they've found the offending luggage.
Mr. and Mrs. Baxter are missing.
Another passenger discrepancy has been identified.
They've put more fuel in the tank—*There are*

no filling stations between JFK and LAX
says Captain Steve. They've checked the IDs
of every passenger on board and every passenger not,
Mr. and Mrs. Baxter still nowhere to be found.

But Captain Steve remains confident.
We'll be on our way momentarily. He does not
know what that means. You, for one, hope
you're aloft for longer than that. You've been

looking forward to uninterrupted reading,
a book called *Black Box* that Mr. and Mrs. Baxter
gave you, or maybe just lent, before they didn't
get on the plane. Bruce Starr, unshaven,

is sitting beside you, sound asleep, snoring.
Before nodding off, he wondered if he were
the discrepancy. He looks more like a rock star.
When he wakes up, you'll ask for his autograph.

Tadpole

The initial ascent was gentle. She and her father came quickly to the opening ringed by pines. Sunlight filtered through the branches, mottled the carpet of needles. It was a place she could find peace. She called it *The Cathedral*. Usually they rested there, at the semicircle of boulders that looked like gravestones. She knew that someday she'd kneel before one, scratch her name on it, along with her dates of birth and death, but today she wanted to keep going, and ran, getting her hands sticky from sap as she pushed aside the branches of fir trees that had fallen across the trail during winter. She reached the pond before her father, stooped to scrub her hands in the murky water only to find a skim of ice extending from the edge a few feet into the pond. When her father caught up, he broke it apart with a stick. Several large globs rose to the surface. He prodded one into the coffee can they'd brought—it looked like a soccer ball made of clear gumdrops, a single black seed at the center of each. Back home, she emptied the can into a plastic tub that he'd filled from a nearby brook and placed in the sunniest part of their yard. During the next few weeks, she watched the jelly dissolve, the seeds grow into tadpoles, the tadpoles lose their tails, become frogs. She asked how to tell the girls from the boys. From the outside it's difficult, her father said. You have to look inside. She already had. Even at eight she knew.

The Swan Song of Mr. Bullfrog

If I thought it would make you more pleasant, I'd vote for change this time, but not for anyone you favor, not while you prosper and I suffer at your hand. Can't you show a little concern? You never meant to harm me? You're upset at the blood, surprised it's red? We're not that different. At least you had the decency to nudge me out of sight beneath the junipers. You left me to die, didn't realize that I was only regrouping, waiting for you to leave. Late afternoon: sun, clouds, trees—I'd almost forgotten. I mean, other than the lid being ripped off my world, there was no warning. Don't try to call it self-defense; it's no way to co-exist. You know swimming is what I live for. All I ask is clean water, a little space, and pure air. There I was minding my own business, splashing about in my cold-blooded body, alone, not a care, cruising along, my powerful kick propelling me through the pool where I'd lived all winter undercover in the dark, hearing frightening things I could not see, mostly your damn beagle howling and sniffing around. Though I longed for the patter of rain to touch my skin, at least I was safe. But in this world with a new sky, suddenly there I was, under attack by you, forced to tuck myself under one of those huge white tablets that sting my eyes, sucked into a pipe trying to flush me away with rotting leaves to God-knows-where. You came after me with a stick. Then a weapon with prongs. Give me back the Goddamn fork! you said. What harm had I done? I don't disturb the peace you can't seem to find. I've learned to suppress my croaking at night; I know it's misunderstood. I feast only on what floats by; I rid your life of gnats. Of course I believe in laissez-faire. So yes, you can have your bloody arsenal, but please use it on barbecues, not me. My three-chambered heart can't take much more of those needle-nose pliers that ripped me like a fishhook when you crammed them down my throat. I am not fish. I am not tasty—not even my legs, you fool. They're not chicken. Didn't they teach evolution in school? I lay there gasping and bleeding.

When it turned dark, I crawled out on my belly, crossed the yet-warm flagstone. Thank God I could still swim. Such exquisite pleasure. But again you came. A few swift strokes and I reached bottom—bad luck, the shallow end. My back against the wall, you snagged me in your net and hurled me downhill. Still, I'll have you know: all it's going to take is one giant leap for frogkind and I'll squeeze through your fucking fence. You can't keep us out. I won't be back, but my children will. And their children. A plague of them.

Drought

A long time it has forgotten how to rain,
no grace left, nothing but the old grass roots.
They held on well, but now they must let go,
the well of good intentions run dry.

No grace left, nothing but the old grass roots
on another day the sky is empty,
the well of good intentions run dry
and everyone gone on summer recess.

On another day the sky is empty,
no governor to keep things under control
and everyone gone on summer recess
with temperatures soaring. A system unchecked,

no governor to keep things under control.
Now and then assemblies form
with temperatures soaring. A system unchecked,
and you can hear their thunder

now and then. Assemblies form,
agitate to finally bring some drops of rain,
and you can hear their thunder,
see their underbellies churn charcoal black,

agitate to finally bring some drops of rain.
That threatening yellow-green-purple-gray—
see their underbellies churn charcoal black
clouds that mushroom upward,

that threatening yellow-green-purple-gray
building to a head that might prevail.
Clouds that mushroom upward
refusing to spill, what could you call this?

Building to a head that might prevail,
skies shutting down again, and again
refusing to spill. What could you call this?
This filibuster, how long can it go on,

skies shutting down again and again?
They held on well, but now they must let go
this filibuster. How long can it go on?
A long time. It has forgotten how to rain.

Earthworm

Yesterday's corpses in the war, and today's
soon-to-be, littering the driveway—
annelid, common earthworm,
much studied, because there's little chance
of understanding a complex creature
without figuring out a simpler one,

one that manages its way by feel,
sensing light through darkness, groping
for brightness in an ad hoc strategy
for survival in the midst of this drought
of good news. Wouldn't you think
the earthworm would dig deeper

in search of moisture, that it could
resist the temptation of a little
night dew, not rise to the surface
and poke about until it finds pavement,
not start to inch across without knowing
there's a place worth getting to?

When it begins to dry out, lose its
moist pinkness and turn brown, crusty,
when it must sense things aren't going well,
it's too late to turn back, too far
to reach the other side—earthworm,
not far enough along to figure things out.

Yesterday's Questions

—for Bruce

Yesterday's questions began with an apple tree
dropping clusters of still-healthy leaves.
A parching June? Too late the drenching July?
But no—a trio of squirrels
biting off stems and sending them down.

Why this year? Why the apple?
Why gnaw through bark, yet eat no leaves?
Why even ask? Like you, my friend,
I want answers where there are none.

Did the apple turn momentarily sweet
in its whole body, not just the fruit?
The way it turned for your wife,
her cancer stalled by chemicals,
as those squirrels might be,
the thirst for time carrying her until the rains came,
blessed her with a month of lushness.

The how of things is everywhere apparent,
the why nowhere to be found.
I often confuse them.

I think it comes down to this: I answer the how
because I can, but to unscramble the why
we'd have to understand what purpose is served
by having us here, then suddenly gone.

Passion Lies Down

According to the menu, it lies down
on the brownie fudge, a dessert you can eat
only in the mind, until you take
a room at the Grand Hotel CastaDiva Villas.
Here, the patrons are alive and well
sipping Bellinis beside Lago di Como.
Unfit for swimming, they say—
too dirty, cold—but there's a floating pool,
heated, with a teak deck. Passing

boats rock it gently, lap water over the lip,
rearrange pairs of slip-on shoes.
Mouths on the terrace munch carpaccio
smothered in greens and herbed mayonnaise,
discuss things you don't want to hear.
Bottles of Dom Perignon Millesimato
poke from chests of ice, bead up in the sun.
Here, you don't ask the price,
don't worry about another scandal

enveloping a prime minister
like fog beginning to fall over the mountains,
politics alive and well everywhere,
parties locked in death grips without your help,
stocks worth half as much now
as when you booked this trip, but here you are
in the place where passion lies down,
here at the steam bath of your fantasies—
walls tiled in turquoise, pink and white,

swirling notes of Eucalyptus,
tropical-rain and summer-storm scented
showers, waterfalls to loosen the neck,
serpentine chaise in a room lined with blocks
of salt carved from deep sea caves.
Anything to make it lie down for a while.
Today is today. Here, you don't think
about tomorrow when serenity
will have seemed more imaginary than real

as you descend through clouds,
bump to a stop, and reach for the phone
in your pocket. There you'll feel
that oddly shaped leaf you plucked
from the tree laden with miniature acorns,
more holly than oak, the kind you've seen
only in a place high up and far away.
It will crumble to dust, momentary
memento of a time briefly held, then spent.

Ode to a Martini

. . . the only American invention
as perfect as the sonnet.
—H.L. Mencken

In training, eight of us, the day before
National Martini Day, already
ruddy from white wine, watch the maestro pour
a splash of Scotch, flavor the rocks, steady
his hand, restrain the ice, drain the pitcher,
then drizzle the gin. We debate how dry
to craft it, how close vermouth's encounter
should be. Just pass the uncapped bottle by,
says one. We settle on a drop apiece,
agree to stir, not shake, drink from the same
giant goblet, make the seeming caprice
a serious toast to friendship, not a game,
no trifling lark, but something well beyond—
we let this crisp concoction build a bond.

Figure Skating

Ever think about how we figure skate
through life? Not so much the hard spills, the cuts
and bruises from which we pick ourselves up,
but those long interludes in the program
meant to set up the key moments—Axels,
Salchows—whether to make them doubles
or triples or the occasional quad.
So much depends on the leaps—the take off,
the time aloft, the sureness of the landing—
that we hardly work on the rest. And when
we have children, it becomes about how well
we prepare them for their big moments,
what we accomplish during the stretch
between their arrival and our departure.
How we hold position in the final spin.

IV. Essay

Absent-Minded Professor Joke: A famous mathematician works in the city at a university and lives with his family in the suburbs. One day they make a short move to a three-story, slate-gray Victorian house with red shutters the next street over, a move his wife oversees while he's at work. He leaves his old house in the morning and returns at the end of the day to the new street, but can't find his new house. So he crosses the boulevard to where a group of boys is playing kickball and says, "A famous mathematician moved here today. Do any of you know where he lives?" and two boys respond, "Sure, Dad, right over there."

Remembrance Day, November 11, 2011—my father laughs hard, a deep, rolling belly laugh, and says, "Yes, I remember telling you that one. Only the shutters were green." He liked to embellish a joke or story or brainteaser, and I learned from him. The mention of young boys takes us back to our childhoods. I get there first. He's much slower these days.

After-School Detention Assignment: Sum the sequence of counting numbers one, two, three, all the way up to a hundred.

I remember my father telling me a story[1] about the famous German mathematician, Carl Friedrich Gauss, Gauss in grade school, a boy commanding a certain power over an adult. The power of a mind. Gauss and his fellow students were detained after class one day for bad behavior and given an assignment to complete before they could leave. He sat quietly at his desk while the other students scratched away and erased their slates. Then, taking his chalk, he scribbled the correct answer and presented it to his astonished teacher. But his teacher knew how he accomplished it, listing in his head all one hundred numbers both forwards and backwards and noticing that the sum of the corresponding entries in each list is always 101: 1 + 100 = 101; 2 + 99 = 101; and so on, up to 100 + 1 = 101. Because each number appears twice, once in each list, the sum of all one hundred numbers is 100 × 101 / 2 = 5,050.

Who could not like that young boy for such cleverness? Who would be surprised that the prodigy went on to wondrous things, plowing his way through the landscape of numbers to discover and invent several big ideas in mathematics? Gauss is the mathematician behind the "bell curve." In the field of probability and statistics, it is known as the "Gaussian" or "normal" distribution. Modern-day Germans' pride in their most famous mathematician was so great that they featured him on their paper currency, the Ten Deutsche Mark note, right until it was discontinued in 1993. Gauss—that's who I wanted to be.

Rowboat Problem: A man rows his boat at two miles per hour against a one-mile-per-hour current. As he begins to perspire, he takes off his cap, throws it into the river, and watches it float away. He keeps rowing upriver for fifteen minutes, then turns the boat around instantly, and, still rowing at two miles per hour, travels downriver until he catches up with his hat. How far downriver has the hat traveled from where it was dropped?

My father, the professor, wanted to leave his mark on the world. The world in his case was the field of physics, and being his older son, my world was tuned to his. He aspired to be a major star and groomed me to follow in his orbit, a minor star subject to his gravitational pull. He started teaching me when I was young, mathematics first because it's the platform on which physics is built, posing little puzzles—brainteasers—to illustrate key principles, each an indelible lesson. He liked rowboat problems, some so difficult they couldn't be called mere brainteasers. One problem involved a fine point in physics he felt he'd dissected so elegantly that he persuaded himself to write up the result and publish it in *Physical Review Letters*. He liked rowboat problems until later in life when he retired and built a house in the Thousand Islands near Lake Ontario. His rowboat, acquired so he could transport his grandchildren to stomp around nearby Milton Island, had a small motor that didn't always work, as it seemed my left brain didn't always work when challenged with one of his math puzzles.

In the middle of our afternoon walk one day when I was eleven, my father posed a simple rowboat problem to highlight the advantage of a good frame of reference, a so-called "word problem" of the type many high school students dread in their algebra courses. At eleven, I hadn't yet studied algebra. He was trying to show me that I could solve a problem without resorting to complicated mathematics and that I should always strive for what he referred to as an "elegant" solution. "You need to learn to solve this type of problem in your head," he said. "Then you'll be able to do that for your homework assignments in math and physics when you go to college. Otherwise, walking to and from class will just be wasted time. You should be able to solve most problems without having to write anything down." Had it been twenty years later, he might have added, "Like Stephen Hawking."

It was the nature of the elegant solution to the rowboat problem more than the problem itself that was instructive that day. After I had pondered it a while without success, my father and I had one of our signature conversations. "This is about frames of reference," he said. "Your head is stuck thinking that all motion must be measured relative to land because land is your everyday frame of reference. That makes the problem harder than it needs to be."

"But you asked how far the hat floated downriver," I said. "Isn't that a distance measured relative to land?"

"Yes, but the man is not on land. While he's in the rowboat, the river is his natural frame of reference. If he stopped rowing, he wouldn't be moving relative to the river. The hat isn't moving relative to the river—

it's merely being carried along by it."

"So you want me to pretend the man is unaware of the land," I said. "The river is his whole world."

"That's right. But recognize that the problem is equivalent to a man walking along a road, taking off his hat and placing it on the ground, then walking away from it for fifteen minutes before turning around and walking back to pick it up. It doesn't matter how quickly or slowly he walks, as long as he always travels the same speed."

"Oh, I see," I said. "Because it takes him exactly fifteen minutes from when he puts down his hat to when he turns around, it must take him exactly fifteen minutes from when he turns around to when he reaches the hat, and that's true regardless of his speed, as long as he walks at a constant pace."

"Correct. Can you solve the problem now?" my father asked.

"It's easy," I said. "To the man in the rowboat, the surface of the river is precisely the same as the road is to the man on land. The man in the rowboat also spends a total of thirty minutes separated from his hat. Since the river flows at one mile per hour relative to the land, the hat travels half a mile downriver." I beamed. I had solved the problem, albeit with my father's prodding and assistance, but completely in my head the elegant way. As a boy, I had no idea a day would come when I would be the one telling the jokes and posing the puzzles.

Inscription in a Physics Text: To Jim with thanks for many contributions to the book. Dad. October 10, 1976.

So well did my father know how the physical world worked it seemed as if he'd made all the rules and assembled it himself. He was able to explain complicated concepts in a variety of ways. If one didn't penetrate, another invariably would. I never saw him perform as professor, but I'm sure that students who started one of his college courses without an interest in physics soon developed one, the subject inevitably more exciting when he paraded around the front of the class. After fifteen years teaching from other people's textbooks, about which he grumbled incessantly (ultimately burning my high school physics text in the fireplace), he decided to write one of his own. He ended up writing three. Two were collaborations with a long-time colleague, the first covering standard topics for a freshman course and the second more sparing in its reliance on mathematics—he'd wanted to title that one *Physics for Poets,* but the publisher vetoed the idea. The third was a solo effort, an opus to compete with the highly successful text by Halliday & Resnick that commanded a huge share of the market. With *University Physics for Science and Engineering,*[2] my father succeeded at putting his name on something important and getting many tens of thousands of students to notice. The text was translated into several languages. For nearly ten years it was a force in the college market and its several editions earned him hundreds of thousands of dollars in royalties, a useful supplement to his modest stipend as a government employee at a military institution.

Recently I retrieved a copy of that 864-page text from my library, now filled with hundreds of books of contemporary poetry and thousands of other works of literature. I hadn't looked at my father's tome in more than thirty years. In the preface, he thanks my mother for typing the manuscript and for assisting with many other aspects of its preparation. That would be as close as she would ever allow herself to approach the subject of physics, typing symbols she didn't understand on an IBM Selectric, changing the typeballs to make summation and integral signs and partial derivatives, a language she couldn't speak. During those years, she devoted her time to transform my father's scratchings into elegant typeface. It was painstaking work. In that preface, my father does not thank me for laboring over the galley proofs to check the myriad equations, nor for the hundreds of hours of freelance work I provided in solving all the end-of-chapter problems, not only the odd-numbered ones, the answers to which would appear at the back of the text as a courtesy to students, but also the even-numbered ones, because they would be included in the teacher's handbook that accompanied the text. My father referred to these as "worked problems," and I was paid a dime for each. That amounted to an average of about $3 per chapter and $150 for the entire book. He drove a hard bargain. It was not good pay, even for the mid-1970s, the only sub-minimum-wage work I ever performed, actually filial duty more than work, a repayment of all the hours of nurture he'd invested in me.

Before returning the book to its spot on my shelves, I turned to the title page and found my father's inscription. That was as close to a hug as I'd get from him. In later years when I visited my parents with my wife and children, our partings were always the same—a hug from my mother and a handshake from my father while he turned his head down and away, unable to make eye contact. We've learned to joke about it. But I noticed it wasn't just me to whom my father was uncomfortable revealing his emotions. I've never seen him display affection for my mother, not a light kiss, an arm around her waist, or even a hand on her shoulder. That affection must have always existed, demonstrated in other ways or in private, because she's supported him throughout their long marriage. And for me, she's provided the tangible and intangible hugs I counted on, yet almost always took for granted.

Pythagorean Theorem: The square of "drive" plus the square of "ambition" equals the square of "obsession," a certain kind of madness rooted in a sense of inadequacy.

My father and I often hiked the mountains of the Eastern Townships. Armed with compass and topographical maps, Canadian-government-issued 1:50,000-scale renderings from aerial photographs, we would set out in search of tiny unnamed ponds he could call his own. He'd always wanted to own a pond or island somewhere, a place he could affix his name to for all time. On those days, even as the sun set early behind the mountains, we'd stand at the edge of his latest discovery, linger until there was barely sufficient time to make it back to the car before dark. Then hurrying along, we'd slip on moss-covered rocks in brooks and scramble through brambles as night squeezed the last light from the forest. We'd talk about his conquest on the drive home and share the exhilaration.

As driven as he was to find those ponds, my father was more interested in being identified with accomplishments in mathematics or physics. His 1951 doctoral dissertation, *High Energy Nuclei Emitted under Proton Bombardment*, reported the results of experiments he'd conducted using a particle accelerator known as a synchrotron in which charged particles are driven to higher and higher energies traveling round and round in a circle, held in that trajectory by a magnetic field adjusted to increase in strength as the particles increase in energy. During his grad school years, while working summers at General Electric's research facilities in Schenectady, he built one of the first prototypes of synchrotrons used to accelerate protons, work that led to three design patents. My father was a natural experimentalist, but part theoretician too; I am a pure theoretician, preferring to remain stuck in my head than dirty my hands in a lab. Through a variety of home experiments, including constructing a cloud chamber to detect cosmic rays, he tried to excite me in experimental work. I was always intrigued with what he built and how he built it, but was more interested in writing down the equations for why it worked. Equations are a theoretician's crutch.

My father claimed that one of his early research papers should have won him a Nobel Prize, but a journal referee rejected the paper, then stole the results, published them under his own name and was later awarded a Nobel. The matter sounds like sour grapes, and perhaps it was, but whether reality or delusion, it bothered him for a long time. Etched into his brain, it became a truth that caused him to strive for some other achievement to establish his name, something high-profile, usually due to its purported impossibility, though he'd refuse to acknowledge that until his efforts proved fruitless. It compelled him to try to find an isolated quark and a magnetic monopole. He, among others, chased the illusion of room-temperature fusion. When everything else failed, he turned to a famous, long-standing mathematical conjecture and pinned his hopes of lasting fame on providing an elegant proof.

It's hard to chase talent lying so far out in the tail of the probability distribution, talent so rare it occurs less frequently than one in a million, a Gauss or an Einstein. Though generally straightforward in mathematics to discern when a boundary has been crossed, it's not so easy when it comes to people, a fine line between a healthy drive to discover and an obsessive need to make a large impact on the world. Both my father and I have struggled to avoid crossing that line. I can't say that either of us succeeded.

Euler's Identity: $e^{i\pi} + 1 = 0$

We had flown to Windsor from all parts of Canada, the top three from each province in the annual high school mathematics competition—Windsor, home to a salt mine and birthplace of Canada's largest salt manufacturer, Canada's southernmost city, lying on the south bank of the Detroit River across from Detroit. It was 1967, the year I graduated from high school. I can't remember the month, but there was still snow on the ground and no leaves on the trees. It was cold.

Before leaving for the conference, all attendees had been told there would be a lecture on game theory. None of us knew much about the subject. That was decades before John Nash won the Nobel Prize in Economics for his application of game theory to the problem of competitive market equilibrium. Before Sylvia Nasar had written her book, *A Beautiful Mind*.[3] Before that award-winning book had been made into an Oscar-winning movie. As our introduction to game theory, we'd been told to be prepared to discuss strategy for the Chinese game of Nim. We'd been given a particular version of the game to solve: three rows of pennies—three in the top row, five in the middle row, and seven in the bottom row. Two players alternate turns. Each turn involves a player selecting a row and picking up and discarding as many pennies from that row, and only that row, as he likes, but always at least one penny. The game continues until all pennies have been picked up. The player to take the last one loses the game. Hours of competitive entertainment for only fifteen cents. Our assignment was to figure out the winning strategy, including whether it is optimal to have the first turn. The keynote lecture, to be given by a mathematics professor from the University of Windsor, would analyze the general game of Nim with any number of rows and any number of pennies in each row—admission for would-be mathematicians only.

The language of that weekend at Windsor was mathematics. I no longer remember the keynote lecture except that the winning strategy for Nim involves representing the number of pennies in each row in base two, everything zeroes and ones. Like "machine code" for computers, everything either off or on. Everyone was on that weekend, but nobody bothered to play a game of Nim—we'd all solved it by the time of the conference, and like tic-tac-toe, it's boring when the outcome is known at the outset.

During the informal welcoming talk, our faculty host asked if any of us knew an equation that links five numbers fundamental to mathematics: 0, 1, e, i, and π. I was the first to blurt out the answer: "Euler's identity, a special case of Euler's formula." The professor asked how I knew it, and I said my father had shown me. Even without knowing how to derive it, one can see that it's a magnificent result. What strange bedfellows the three numbers e, i, and π: e associated with "exponential" growth, i a so-called "imaginary" number, and π the stuff of circles. Peeling away that strangeness involves understanding so-called "complex" numbers, part real and part imaginary; in particular, the subset of complex numbers lying on the circumference of a circle with radius one centered at the origin of the complex plane. Euler's formula represents all points on that circle, and his identity results from a tour exactly halfway around. My father said I should learn about complex numbers and calculus if I wanted to derive Euler's formula. No time better than my senior year in high school. He always wanted me to get ahead and stay there. With a hunger for learning new things and for being the best, I did not resist. Sometimes my drive was catalyzed by my father's push, but mostly it was an inner pull I felt from the traits he'd passed down.

Zeno's Paradox: A woman stands 200 feet from a wall. She performs a series of ever-shorter walks straight toward the wall, first moving 100 feet closer, then 50, then 25, each time halving the distance remaining. There is an infinite number of stages in her walk. Will she ever get there?

Infinite series, my father told me, provide one of the elegant ways to prove Euler's formula. He started with the series 1 + ½ + ¼ + . . . , each successive number exactly one-half the number before it. Not all infinite sums add up to a finite number, but this one does. It "converges" to a "limit." In lieu of summing the counting numbers from 1 to 100, Gauss's teacher could have made his students sum this particular series. Because it's infinite, they would have had to sit and think how to solve the problem, realizing they couldn't scratch partial sums on their slates forever. I'm certain that Gauss would have solved it in his head. But thousands of years before Gauss, the Greek philosopher Zeno had already posed his now-famous paradoxes and showed us how.

Zeno knew the woman could walk straight to the wall and reach it in finite time, but, being a philosopher, he looked at the problem a different way and suggested it might take her infinite time because there is an infinite number of stages to her journey. Hence the paradox.

But the paradox is imagined, not real. If the woman pauses to rest for a second after each stage, she'll never get to the wall. But if she doesn't pause, just keeps walking at the same speed, merely taking note of each stage marker as she passes it, those markers bunching closer and closer together, she will arrive at the wall in finite time. If she walks at constant speed, each succeeding stage will take exactly half the time of the previous stage, and the sum of the times for the infinite number of stages will be finite. This little "thought experiment," although not really a paradox, is still useful—it shows how to sum the infinite "geometric series" (a series in which pairs of successive numbers are in constant ratio). In total, the woman travels a distance of 200 feet, equal to the sum of all the stages: first 100 feet, then 50, then 25, and so on. Therefore, 100 + 50 + 25 + . . . = 200. Dividing each term by 100, one obtains 1 + ½ + ¼ + . . . = 2.

Train Problem: There are two trains 200 miles apart heading toward each other on the same track, each traveling at a speed of 50 miles per hour. A crazed bee, which always flies at 150 miles per hour, leaves the front of one of the trains and flies straight toward the other. When it reaches the second train, it turns around instantly and flies back toward the first, continuing this behavior until it is finally crushed between the two crashing trains. How far does the bee fly before its death?

"It's an infinite series," I said.

"It is indeed," my father said, "and there was a famous mathematician at a cocktail party trying to pick up a woman in a red dress. He had just handed her an extra-dry martini when he was interrupted in his flirtation by a friend who posed the train-and-bee problem and dared him to solve it in his head. The mathematician thought for a few seconds, then answered correctly—300 miles—and turned his attention back to the suitably impressed woman."

"Were you the famous mathematician?" I asked.

"Not that time," my father said.

"So how did he solve the problem?"

"He claims to have solved it exactly as anybody else would have, recognizing that it was Zeno's paradox in disguise. He summed the series in his head."

"Zeno's paradox?"

"Of course," my father said. "The bee flies for an hour until it meets the oncoming train. At that point the trains are only 100 miles apart, exactly half the original distance. So the bee will fly half an hour after turning around, then a quarter of an hour after turning around again, and so on. The infinite series is $1 + \frac{1}{2} + \frac{1}{4} + \ldots$"

"Which sums to two," I said. "The bee flies for two hours before the trains crash. At 150 miles per hour, that's 300 miles of flying. But why did the mathematician choose to sum the infinite series?—that was the hard way. There is a trivial solution."

"Which is?" my father prodded, and I replied, "Each train travels at 50 miles per hour. They start 200 miles apart and crash at the midpoint—that takes two hours. The bee has been flying the whole time at 150 miles per hour. You don't need to sum an infinite series."

"Right, but when you're smart enough, you can solve it the clumsy way," my father said. "Still, you should never do work you don't have to. It's a waste."

"And inelegant," I added, having the last word.

Problem #8: Prove that any permutation on a finite set can be expressed as a product of a finite number of pairwise disjoint cycles, and that the cycle decomposition is unique.

Without ever explicitly saying so, my father expected me to perform well, whether it was winning the 100-yard dash in a track meet or acing an exam. So it was no surprise when he wondered why I'd only placed third in the province in the high school mathematics competition. After all, this was the same father who used to reward me with a quarter for every perfect 100 on my high school report card, a dime for every 99, and a nickel for every 98, nothing else worth a payment. Thankfully, Sun Life of Canada, a sponsor of the national mathematics competition, saw it differently. They awarded me a scholarship to a Canadian college of my choice. I chose McGill, my father's alma mater, where he earned both his bachelor's and doctorate. Like my father, I chose to pursue an honors degree in physics, but two incidents made me wonder whether I should have chosen mathematics instead.

The first occurred immediately after freshman year. I was looking forward to eight idle weeks before leaving for summer camp to serve as counselor and sailing instructor. My father viewed the gap as an opportunity to get a head start on sophomore year. He suggested I work through the texts for my fall courses in Real Analysis and Electricity & Magnetism. I could read and work problems in the morning, and we could discuss the material in the afternoon while playing golf. I never knew if he was looking forward more to talking mathematics and physics or playing golf. He was a little surprised at how effortlessly I cruised through both texts, more surprised at my relative excitement over the math, and astonished that my already bad golf game actually worsened during those two months. He suggested there was a "conservation law" at play, the sum of my abilities in physics and golf remaining constant through time. He might have been right. Later in life my golf game improved dramatically.

The second incident occurred right after the summer break. Most of the honors students in math and physics had signed up for the sophomore course in Abstract Algebra, taught for the first time by Professor Wilbur Jonsson, reputedly better suited to instructing graduate students than undergraduates. On the first day of class he handed out an assignment with eight problems and said he wouldn't hold lectures for a week. Instead, he wanted us to work on those problems—independently, not together, so he could assay the quality of students in his class. He left after only five minutes.

Thanks to my father, I had already completed the work for two of my courses and could devote nearly all my time to tackle the assignment. I solved the first four problems the day we received them, spent the next day figuring out the fifth, the following two days completing solutions for the sixth and seventh, giving myself three days to deal with the last. Then for two days I made no progress. Pages and pages of crumpled paper filled my wastebasket, which the cleaning lady in my dorm forgot to empty, an annoying reminder that I wasn't getting anywhere. On Sunday, I awoke early and worked until the cafeteria opened. I had a fresh approach to the problem that solidified over breakfast. By noon, things were looking good. By late afternoon, everything had fallen apart. By dinner, I was in despair. I took an early evening walk up Mount Royal to the lookout in the park, returning by dusk to start work again. By two o'clock Monday morning, I had fashioned a multi-page proof I thought held together. Good thing—I'd been up for nineteen hours. I set my alarm and went to bed.

Professor Jonsson arrived five minutes late on Monday. He collected our assignments and said, as he walked out the door, that our first lecture would be Wednesday. On Wednesday, he dropped the stack of graded assignments on the desk at the front of the room, then lifted the top one from the pile and started to examine it. "Most of you solved one problem successfully," he said. "Several of you got two, a few three, one person four and one five. A solid effort—these are very difficult problems." He held up the assignment he'd been looking through and waved it in front of the class. "One of you solved all eight problems, and only that person provided a complete proof for problem #8. It is a result from Group Theory known as the Cycle Decomposition Theorem. I teach the standard proof to my graduate students. Now I have a new, different proof to show them. It's cumbersome, but original. Who did this work?" No one raised a hand. "Whoever it was, please stay after class." I was the one to remain. He tried to persuade me to join the honors program in mathematics. After a week considering it and a phone call home, I decided to stay in physics.

Three years later, in 1971, I graduated from McGill with first-class honors in physics, then left Canada and headed to the United States, where I earned a doctorate at Harvard in 1975 for a thesis in theoretical solid-state physics, *The Effects of Spin-Orbit Interactions in Itinerant Ferromagnets,* a topic in the backwaters of the field, not forefront and mainstream as my father's thesis had been in its time. In a sense, I had surrendered, maybe even sold out. Early in graduate school, I'd concluded I wouldn't continue in academe. Studying under world-renowned professors and alongside graduate students who would one day take their place, I realized I'd never win a Nobel Prize in physics or Fields Medal in mathematics. That pond was too big. I needed to find a smaller one to call my own. One in which I could earn enough to support a lifestyle to which I'd been introduced by a few well-heeled graduate-school friends—the world of restaurants, museums, theater, and the symphony. Art galleries. Weekends on Cape Cod. Country clubs. Trips like my friends' to Paris, London, Rome, and Prague. The non-academic world, in which the real currency is money, not ideas, or if ideas, at least making good money from the best ones.

Coin Problem: There are twelve coins of which eleven are genuine and one is counterfeit. The counterfeit coin is of different weight, but you don't know whether it is lighter or heavier than the genuine coins. You are given a two-pan balance and have to show, in merely three weighings, how to isolate the counterfeit coin and determine whether it is lighter or heavier.

Having decided not to pursue a career in physics and mathematics, yet knowing nothing about the business world, I decided that I needed to find a job in which I could parlay my mathematical skills into a solid career. Sun Life of Canada, based in Montreal, had recently opened its

U.S. headquarters in Wellesley, a western suburb of Boston. Doctoral degree in hand, I approached them about a position as an actuarial trainee, reminding them that they'd provided me a scholarship to attend McGill. During the job interview, I was given the coin problem and asked how I would proceed to solve it. I had some useful ideas, but wasn't able to complete the solution in my head on the spot. They offered me a position anyway, conditional on sending them the full solution and passing the first two actuarial exams. It was good luck and good timing on my part—my bank account was down to its last few hundred dollars, my scholarships had run out, and I was reluctant to ask my father for living money, having never done that.

I did solve the mathematical puzzler and pass those exams. I had found my pond. I completed the rest of the actuarial exams and earned my designation as Fellow of the Society of Actuaries in 1977, but I soon became restless. The pond was too small. I joined the much larger John Hancock Mutual Life Insurance Company in Boston, and, while holding down my day job there, began to think about the relationship between a financial institution's assets and its liabilities. The two sides of an insurance company's balance sheet are managed by different parts of the organization. Back then, there was little coordination between them. It had occurred to me that spiking interest rates could render the life insurance industry insolvent. On short notice, policyholders could surrender their life insurance and annuity policies and withdraw their cash values to invest elsewhere at much higher returns. With asset portfolios at depressed market values, insurers might not be able to pay. It happened that I was right—the insurance industry was in severe financial distress in the late 1970s, no large company more so than The Equitable Life Assurance Society of the United States (such grand names insurers gave themselves) in New York City where I went to work after they offered me double what I was earning at The Hancock.

At Equitable, I lived a political nightmare for two years, heading a small group of actuaries responsible for analyzing the financial condition of the company's pension products line of business. Every one of our reports landed on company management like an atomic bomb. The news finally made its way to the board of directors. A business that had appeared profitable for many years was on the verge of yielding over a billion dollars in losses during the next five years. Fortunately, I'd made friends with my counterpart on the investment side of the house who managed the multi-billion dollar asset portfolio supporting the pension liabilities. He tossed me a lifeline and pulled me across the street to Morgan Stanley, which he'd recently joined to establish a fixed-income research department. My wife, previously a stockbroker, played no small part in getting me to move, pointing out that the head of fixed-income research at First Boston was earning a seven-figure income. Morgan Stanley didn't offer me that kind of money, but did double my pay. I was making "powers of two" work for me, exponential growth in compensation that would happily continue for a while.

Branch in a Decision Tree: My father kept telling me: "To choose is to eliminate. Don't look back and regret the choices you've made." One of those times I should have asked: "Can you regret a choice your father made?"

At Morgan Stanley, I'd found not another pond, but a lake, if not a great lake. I was one of Wall Street's first "rocket scientists," ironically without any real experience working as a mathematician or physicist—not like the true rocket scientists the Street hired in earnest beginning in the mid-1980s. Still, I was fortunate to be a "quant" (a mathematical jock) at the time they came into favor. When my boss retired, I became global head of fixed-income research and stayed in that position for a few years. Then I took a tour of duty in investment banking to advise Property & Casualty insurers on managing their earthquake and hurricane exposure. My product development group engineered "catastrophe bonds" through which insurers could lay off risk to a broad pool of institutional investors. I ended my working career as Chief Information Officer for four years, retiring at age fifty in early 2001.

While holding down those various positions at Morgan Stanley, I kept writing research papers because I enjoyed it. A few won prizes, one for my work on catastrophe bonds and another for demonstrating how Monte Carlo simulation (a fancy name for the computer-generated equivalent of the random outcomes of spinning a roulette wheel) can be used to price American put options. A put option is a security that gives its owner the right to sell a share of stock at a specified price. The label "American" is used to distinguish the exercise right from the "European" kind. The holder of a European put option can exercise his right to sell only at expiration of the contract, whereas the holder of an American option can exercise his right any time up to and including expiration. The American option is more valuable because exercise before expiration is sometimes optimal. People had thought it was impossible to utilize Monte Carlo simulation to price American options. In 1994, I published a paper proving otherwise.[4] The inspiration came during a long walk, like those I'd taken with my father thirty years earlier. I was not headed anywhere in particular that morning, just needed to get out and clear my mind. Somewhere along the path I happened to discover an algorithm that worked. It involved solving a decision tree by a technique known as "backward induction," a tree in which the branch at each point in time and sampled stock price forks into a choice between exercising the option or not.

On the strength of that paper, I was invited to give the keynote address at a financial economics conference at Queen's University in Kingston, about five miles from where my father had been principal at the Royal Military College (having changed jobs and moved to Ontario from Quebec in 1978, two years after the separatist Parti Québécois came to power and rendered life in Quebec too constraining for many English-speaking Canadians) and fewer than ten miles from my parents' home on the St. Lawrence River. I asked my father to attend the lecture, the first, and likely the only, time he would see me perform in a professional capacity. It did not happen. My parents had already committed to visit my younger brother's family in Denver and were unwilling to alter their plans. We missed each other by a matter of hours. As it turned out, the opportunity never arose again. I've never told my father I thought he made the wrong choice. I would not have made the same decision. When put to the test, I didn't. Some ten years later, though it would have been easier psychologically on both my older son and me for me merely to walk along and watch him compete in the 2005 U.S. Men's Amateur Golf Championship, when he asked me to carry his bag for the tournament, I didn't hesitate. For me, a once-in-a-lifetime opportunity for the benefit of my child trumps all.

I have been asked many times how I would sum up my career. People expect me to say that I've enjoyed a variety of successes. I don't disagree, but I always come back to the irony of finding myself stuck in a loop, destined to repeat the same experience. No matter what I chose to do professionally, I was viewed as too good and not good enough, often at the same time—my research papers considered impenetrable by most of my fellow actuaries but judged insufficiently rigorous by true mathematicians; an investment expert among actuaries, but, without the credentials of an MBA, not a proper investment banker among those who had graduated business school and come up through the corporate ranks. At the end, I was a CIO who sometimes couldn't navigate his own laptop, considered by people on the business side as the right common-sense geek to run a global technology operation, but viewed by the people within it as an outsider. I was an overachiever who hadn't overachieved, someone who could solve all kinds of mathematical puzzles, even legitimate mathematical problems, but who hadn't yet discovered his own Euler formula, a person who couldn't escape the discomfort with life that only his own high standards caused, someone never satisfied with the successes he'd achieved, always craving a greater one. In those things, someone just like his father.

Four-Color Theorem: Four distinct colors suffice to color any map so that no two adjacent countries have the same color.[5]

Prior to retirement, my father's days were overfilled with duties as principal of the Royal Military College, an employee of Canada's Department of National Defence, highest-ranking civil servant in the country, equivalent to a general. So stressful was his job that he suffered a series of serious heart attacks in early 1982, the last while I was away on a business trip. When I arrived at the hospital, I headed straight for the ICU. Coming towards me down a long corridor was a short man in a white coat, dark-complexioned with narrow-set eyes and a handlebar moustache, identical in appearance to a medical student I remembered from McGill who was then an assistant warden in my dorm. He was shocked when I called out his name. After I explained how I knew him, he shook my hand and said the angiogram had gone well but a quadruple bypass was necessary.

"Your father has had multiple heart attacks. He's in bad shape and will lead a highly restricted life if we don't operate, but there are serious risks. His chances are nowhere nearly as good as if the procedure were purely preventative."

"What is the probability he'll make it through surgery?" I asked.

"I wish his chances were better," he replied. I sensed he didn't want to say what he thought my father's chances were. Doctors are not mathematicians. "He's in no position to evaluate his circumstances. You're the one who will have to decide," I was told.

"Are his chances as good as 50-50?" I asked.

"Oh, much better than that," the surgeon said.

"Well then, 75-25?"

"No, better than that."

"So how good are they?"

"They're not as good as I'd like. If he hadn't had any heart attacks, almost 99%, but now only 92%, I'm afraid."

"There's nothing to decide," I said. "Go ahead and operate. In his condition, with no life awaiting him if you don't, 92% is as good as 100%." The surgeon looked as if I were daft. My father had never held the medical profession in high regard. He considered MDs to be glorified cooks who learn how to follow complicated recipes without ever pausing to think. To my father, PhDs were the "real doctors." But he ended up owing his life to this diminutive doctor with expert hands, who had acquired a reputation as the leading heart surgeon in Canada, able to perform complicated procedures much faster than others.

My father soon recovered and returned to his position as principal. He lasted only a year before deciding to retire four months short of his fifty-ninth birthday. I never wondered what he would do after retiring. Though he was finished teaching and running an academic institution, he still had something to prove. He'd clung to the dream of leaving his mark, as if he hadn't already done that during an illustrious career. He decided he needed to prove some famous mathematical conjecture. With so many outstanding problems to work on, he made an odd choice—one that had already been solved.

Why the four-color map problem? Partly because he knew he wouldn't be spending time trying to prove a conjecture that might be false, but mostly because the only known solution was "ugly," relying on a computer to enumerate and analyze thousands of distinct map configurations. My father wanted to prove it by human mind alone. He felt the theorem deserved a more elegant treatment and decided to place his bets on the method of "mathematical induction" (different from the technique of "backward induction" mentioned earlier). Many mathematicians would not consider that elegant. The technique seems like out-and-out cheating because success is achieved without having to show why the result is true. One merely demonstrates that it is and leaves it at that. No insight is gained; the result is not constructed, merely proved. Still, my father had a hunch the inductive proof would turn out to be short, not hundreds of pages, and that would be elegant enough.

Mathematical induction is a technique used to prove the truth of a statement involving an arbitrary positive integer n (a counting number). The proof begins by showing the statement is true for some starting value of n, say n = 1. The inductive step involves assuming the statement is true for an arbitrary value of n and proving that it must then also be true for n+1. The combination of the two steps means that the statement is true for n = 1, then necessarily true for n = 2, 3, and so on. Therefore, it is true for all n.

My father assumed the four-color theorem to be true for an arbitrary number of countries n in an arbitrary map. He then set about to prove that the theorem remained true no matter how another country was added to the map. Actually he tended to start with an arbitrary n-country map and subtract a country to get a smaller map. Unlike most other mathematicians who had tried their hand at the problem, my father focused on the countries at the outer boundary of the map, not interior countries. And he focused on strings of adjacent countries that began and ended with a boundary country, strings that partitioned the map into two parts. Day after day he'd fill scraps of paper with diagrams. Many nights he'd go to bed claiming to have solved the problem, so confident at times that he'd e-mail me the news and an outline of his method. Within a few hours I'd develop a counterexample and reply. Most often, however, he awakened to the realization that his latest approach was flawed, sometimes curably he thought, sometimes fatally he'd acknowledge later, in either case no need to read my refutation.

When I visited my parents in the Thousand Islands, my father and I would stand at river's edge and discuss his efforts. We did this while my first marriage crumbled and after I'd entered into my second. My first wife was irritated at our captivation—one that excluded her and the rest of the family—especially when our conversations devolved into heated arguments on technical points, both of us facing the river, not each other. My second wife didn't understand the nature of our arguments either, but was intrigued by what had captured my father in its firm grip and deeply saddened by his obsessive pursuit of the immortality he thought this proof would bestow. Still, my wives and I were merely visitors. My mother lived with the man who had become the four-color problem, and in his retirement there was no escape for her.

In my retirement I had taken up writing poetry. Two of the poems in my book, *In Confidence,*[6] concern my father's plight. An excerpt from the first, "No Two Countries," characterizes the obsession. I had intended it as a description of my father's predicament, but it applied to me as well, because, for a span of a little more than a year, I too couldn't live outside the mathematics.

> *Along the border of sanity, he knows*
>
> *there's always somewhere he can add*
> *or subtract a country, the mathematician*
> *become Van Gogh, mind confined,*
> *coloring to extinction while coloring*
>
> *to stay alive.*

The second of the poems, "Half-Finished Bridge," is based on Bashō's haiku, *first snow falling on the half-finished bridge.* It expresses a hope that my father and I would figure out the problem together.

> *. . . writing to my father*
> *that I'm grateful he's still alive*
> *and there's time to erect the rest of the trestle*
> *and walk together to the other side,*
> *light snow falling on our backs.*

My father's fever of concentration on his inductive proof was so fierce that I began to wonder whether our lives were heading towards a remake of David Auburn's Pulitzer Prize-winning play, *Proof.*[7] With the benefit of several years' remove, I recognize that that thought borders on the absurd. Exactly as for the father in *Proof*, my father isn't going to solve the problem in his lifetime. In the play, it is the father's daughter who succeeds, thus launching a controversy about whether it was her work or her father's, whether she was mathematically capable of devising the proof. However, unlike the play, there will be no dispute in my case—I am not capable of solving the four-color theorem by mathematical induction. I'm not sure anybody is. Perhaps Gauss could have. But even he would have had to deal with the perversity that when a map is colored properly, adding or subtracting a country often necessitates re-coloring a large portion of the original map.

At this point, one might ask, "Who cares? What is the magic in four colors? So what if it takes five? Does proving this theorem, elegantly or otherwise, change anything of substance in the world?" The realistic answer is surely "almost nothing," at least for most people. But to a mathematician, the endeavor is like composing a concerto and performing it flawlessly before a packed Carnegie Hall. More satisfying than earning seven figures. The four-color map conjecture was a famous, long-unsolved problem, not with the cachet of the still unproved Riemann's Conjecture or Goldbach's Conjecture or the now-proved Fermat's Last Theorem, but sufficiently intractable to grant instant fame to the provider of an elegant proof. Not for fifteen minutes. Not for a lifetime. Forever. Not with the impact that Einstein's achievements had on the world, but certainly more glorious than having one's name attached to a tiny pond nestled somewhere in a mountain.

My father didn't give up on the problem until his mind gave up on him. I surrendered much earlier. Not because my ambition to be a bright star in the firmament of mathematics had dulled, but because I had begun to suspect that one might more easily prove that certain theorems involving a countable number of elements are simply not provable by induction. Perhaps my father spent years attempting to prove a known result in a way that wasn't possible. The apparent simplicity of the technique was the allure, a sort of fool's gold, but likely also the fatal mistake. Why did he embark on the journey in the first place? Why did he, as a much younger man, try to discover isolated quarks and magnetic monopoles, chase room-temperature fusion? All in the quest for lasting fame. It can lead one down paths where not even compass and map can help. Perhaps an Einstein or an Euler or a Gauss, talent that is rarer than one in a million, can discover the seemingly impossible, but for the rest of us such a quest is vain, no different from the search for the Holy Grail or the Fountain of Youth. The obsessed mind cannot see the vanity, only the possibility.

Cartoon from The New Yorker Magazine: *A nondescript man at a cocktail party engaged in conversation with a pretty woman says, "Actually, in actuarial circles I'm quite famous."*

Like my father, I have tended to focus on what I haven't accomplished rather than what I have. A telling example dates back to my junior year in high school. I had taken two of the senior-year matriculation exams, both in mathematics, a year early. They were exams administered by Quebec's Department of Education. My grades were 97 for Algebra and 92 for Trigonometry. No money for those results. I was aware of a careless error on a three-point multiple choice question in Algebra, a minus sign I'd missed, but I was sure I had achieved a perfect paper in Trigonometry and wrote the Department to ask them to re-grade my paper, explaining that they had perhaps overlooked my answer to an eight-point question involving a graph. I don't know if they followed up on my request, but I received a politically correct response, which I'm sure I'll be able to retrieve from my memory banks long after most everything else has become inaccessible. They said, "Our goal is to assess a candidate's strengths, not diagnose his weaknesses. We start from zero and measure upward. We do not start from 100 and count down. You should be pleased that you scored 92 on the exam, not upset that you lost eight points." I told my father I wouldn't touch the trigonometry text during my senior year. I would retake the exam without studying. As the date approached, he became irritated with my obstinacy because it forced me to sit for two important exams in a single day—Trigonometry in the morning and Physics in the afternoon. Because I had already scored 92 on Trigonometry, he thought that performing well in Physics was more important than wearing myself out trying to prove a point. I'd be proving it only to myself. I ignored him and earned a perfect 100 on each exam. My mother told me she was proud of my performance on the matriculation exams, second overall in the province, and said that she'd never had a 100 on a final exam. My father didn't seem to care. He'd expected more. "What about Geometry and Intermediate Algebra?" he asked. Having just returned from summer camp, about to head to McGill, and bragging about having had my first beers—underage—I hoped he might break out a few to celebrate. "Pretty good," he said. He handed me the official transcript and asked how the sailing had been.

For people like my father and me, the failure to achieve a greater goal undermines what has already been accomplished. Not living up to self-imposed expectations can have the positive effect of making one more determined or it can have the negative effect of devaluing what might otherwise be viewed as a significant success. Another fine line. In 2008, seven years into my retirement, I received a phone call from the International Insurance Society that they'd named me winner of the Beckley Founders' Award for my pioneering role in developing a methodology for asset-liability management. But who, except for a previous winner of that medal, has ever heard of the Beckley Award? It's not a Nobel Prize or Fields Medal.

I know the Beckley Award counted more to my father than it did to me. His older son, once the little star, had become a big one. Though he felt proud of my accomplishment, and told me so, I could tell that he no longer felt like a star at all, and it wasn't only in his own eyes that he didn't measure up. His whole life he competed with his brother, whose academic achievements were constantly lauded by their father. He says his mother occasionally offered praise but his father didn't seem to notice. To this day, my father carries the burden of his brother's perfect 100 on Ontario's senior matriculation exam in Algebra, the only perfect paper in the subject across the province that year. He still tells the story. Even in the fracturing world of his late-in-life dementia.

When my father accepted his first job after earning his doctorate from McGill, an assistant professorship at Collège Militaire Royal, his father wasn't present to pass judgment, having died shortly before. Instead, his mother stepped in and asked why he hadn't taken a position at a "real university, like University of Toronto," a question she continued to press throughout his career at Canada's two principal military colleges. Perhaps my father's drive to make a mark was not only to prove something to himself but also to outdo his brother and impress his mother. Most likely, though, it was just to impress the world at large. All else would follow. That's the way it has been, and still is, for me.

Mountain Problem: There is a trail up a mountain. You leave the base camp at eight in the morning and reach the summit cabin at eight at night, spend the night there, then start back down at eight the next morning. You take your time, pause to pick berries, lie down and gaze at clouds, and you reach the base camp at eight that night. Prove that there is at least one point in time when you're at the same point on the trail each day.

As my father gets closer to gathering his thoughts about his childhood this Remembrance Day morning, I remember an afternoon when I was a teenager hiking in the mountains with him, both of us growing frustrated in our attempt to find another of his ponds. We were not lost, but seemed not to be in the right place. Or perhaps the pond wasn't. As we sat on a rock staring at the map, he tried to make light of our confusion, or at least distract from it, by posing the mountain problem, turning a challenge of topography into one of topology. As always, his puzzler of the moment wasn't difficult but required a leap of insight because he wouldn't settle for a clumsy solution. I couldn't have said: "Draw two graphs in the x-y plane. Let the x-axis represent time of day and the y-axis distance along the trail measured from the base camp. One graph represents my position on the way up, the other on the way down. Because the graphs must be continuous, they have to intersect." It's a valid argument but wouldn't have passed muster. Instead, I had to recognize that the problem he'd posed is equivalent to the problem in which two different people start at the same time, one at the bottom heading up, the other at the top heading down, both reaching their destinations at the same time. There is no way they can avoid meeting somewhere along the path. Q.E.D. That solution qualifies. And with that clever solution, as for the rowboat problem, one realizes that some of the information is not needed, at least not in the form stated. The two are destined to meet even if they don't start or finish at the same time, as long as neither ever wanders off the path and there is a common interval of time when neither has completed his hike.

The way I now prefer to describe the elegant solution is that the two hikers are father and son. The son starts at the bottom and the father at the top. The son can't help but meet the father somewhere along his journey. This morning we've met at a place where my father doesn't remember the problem or the time in the woods that gave rise to it. I know he won't remember how to solve it; I spare him the embarrassment. Instead, he finally remembers an incident from his childhood, and tells me, as if for the first time, about the day he and his brother met after school at a field near their home, a field of brush they set on fire using their father's magnifying glass, the one they'd "borrowed" from his antique desk, the desk into which my father had once carved his brother's initial trying to get him into trouble. My father recalls the town's sole fire truck extinguishing the flames. He recalls the punishment. And the mischievous streak he never outgrew.

This morning he remembers his Shakespeare and his Shelley, the play *Henry V* and the poem "Ozymandias." He remembers Yeats's widening gyre and a rough beast slouching toward Bethlehem. In prep school he committed them all to memory without effort. They're still retrievable. Sitting in his recliner after breakfast before donning his RCAF uniform and medals for the eleven o'clock memorial service, any thoughts of four colors and mathematics remote from his disjointed mind, he asks if I know *Henry V*'s Saint Crispin's Day speech, *We few, we happy few, we band of brothers.* I let him continue, word for word to the end, pausing only for proper punctuation. Perfect, just as in his school days. Blue ribbon. "Good, Dad," I say, "but that was the Battle of Agincourt. Today commemorates Armistice Day, the end of World War I." He embarks on Lieutenant Colonel John McCrae's poem, "In Flanders Fields," nearly choking on the words, . . . *We are the Dead. Short days ago, we lived, felt dawn, saw sunset glow* . . . I almost ask, "Can the dead be happy?" but catch myself.

In his increasingly complex world, my father wanders from Flanders Fields back to Agincourt and begins to recite Saint Crispin's Day again. "He won't stop," my mother says. "He's been doing this for weeks." "Don't mind him, Mom," I say. "He's alive and happy as Henry the Fifth. He's king." The path, gentle at first, has become a rapid descent. My father has almost made it back to the base camp. I like to think I'm still climbing.

References

[1] E.T. Bell, *Men of Mathematics*, Simon and Schuster, Inc. (1937).

[2] Donald E. Tilley, *University Physics for Science and Engineering*, Cummings Publishing Company, Inc. (1976).

[3] Sylvia Nasar, *A Beautiful Mind: A Biography of John Forbes Nash, Jr., Winner of the Nobel Prize in Economics, 1994*, Simon and Schuster, Inc. (1998).

[4] James A. Tilley, "Valuing American Options in a Path Simulation Model," TSA Volume XLV, The Society of Actuaries (1994).

[5] Robin Wilson, *Four Colors Suffice*, Penguin Group, Penguin Books, Ltd. (2002).

[6] Jim Tilley, *In Confidence*, Red Hen Press (2011).

[7] David Auburn, *Proof: A Play*, Faber and Faber (2001).

Biographical Note

Jim Tilley earned a doctorate in physics from Harvard and worked on Wall Street for twenty years. His first collection of poetry, *In Confidence,* was published by Red Hen Press in 2011. His poems have been published in literary journals such as *Virginia Quarterly Review, The Southern Review, Southwest Review,* and *Alaska Quarterly Review.* He has won the *Sycamore Review*'s Wabash Prize for Poetry, the New England Poetry Club's Firman Houghton Award, and an International Publication Award from *Atlanta Review.* He lives in Bedford Corners, New York.